Young Animals

by Lynn Trepicchio

Harcourt

Orlando   Boston   Dallas   Chicago   San Diego

Visit *The Learning Site!*

www.harcourtschool.com

During the spring some animals are born. The young are cared for.

Every animal is different.
Each animal has
different needs.

Even wild animals care for their young. Some stay with their mothers for a long time.

Other newborns come
out and find their way all
by themselves.

Some animals are born
live. They do not hatch
from eggs.

Other animals hatch
from eggs. Both of these
young animals are ready
to see the world.

Animals need care
before they are born.
Some fathers take care
of their eggs.

Most of the time,
animals wait. That's
what they do the most.

Animals know what their newborns need. They need to learn about the world.

They need to learn to
take care of themselves.
When they are ready,
they will live on their own.

Animal Names

Animal	Young
bear	cub
cat	kitten
duck	duckling
rabbit	bunny
pig	piglet
horse	foal
chicken	chick